No Name in the Street

A Play in One Act

by Edward Murch

Baker's Plays
7611 Sunset Blvd.
Los Angeles, CA 90042
bakersplays.com

First Performances

STAGE

No Name in the Street was first presented by The Y.W.C.A. Players of Plymouth on 16th March, 1966, and subsequently presented by them at The Paignton and South West of England Festival, 1966, when they were awarded the supreme trophy of the Festival for the Best Performance on Drama Winners' Night. These were the players: Kathleen Nixon, Valerie Carbines, Fiona Walker, Margaret Smale, Anne Ware, Rosalind Ducat, Catherine Hunt, Brenda Taylor and Beverly Branch.

The Play was directed by the Author and Helen Rowett

CHURCH

The first church presentation was given by The Concord Society in The Congregational Church, Uxbridge on Good Friday, 1966.

The play was directed by Jean Hobson and John Wright

TELEVISION

The play, featuring members of The Caravan Players, *(Administrators Eleanor and James Green)* was first produced for television by TELERAD, South Central Pennsylvania Television and Radio Ministry *(Don Zechman, Program Co-ordinator)* in co-operation with WGAL-TV (Channel 8) in Lancaster, Pennsylvania U.S.A. on Palm Sunday, 7th April, 1974.

RADIO

A radio version of the play featuring players from The Rutland A.T.S. *(director Lynn Cooper)* was first broadcast by B.B.C. Radio Leicester on Good Friday, 1982.

Radio production was by Janet Mayo.

For
H.G.Q.R.
Master of Many Arts

CHARACTERS

FIRST SPECTATOR
SECOND SPECTATOR
THIRD SPECTATOR
FOURTH SPECTATOR
FIFTH SPECTATOR
MOTHER
TEMPLE TRADER
WIDOW
MISTRESS
SERVANT
FIRST ANGEL
SECOND ANGEL
KITCHENWOMAN
PROPHETESS

By the interchanging of parts the play may be performed by casts of eight to fourteen players as shewn in the Production Notes.

SCENE

In and around Jerusalem during Holy Week

The play is performed in a curtain set.

His remembrance shall perish from the earth, and he shall have no name in the street.

The Book of Job

NO NAME IN THE STREET

(When the play begins the stage is empty then the FIRST SPECTATOR *enters up right, and comes to slightly above right centre.)*

First Spectator. All these years to the day since Jesus died. *(The* SECOND SPECTATOR *enters down left.)*

Second Spectator. All these years to the day since his case was tried —
(The THIRD SPECTATOR *enters down right.)*

Third Spectator. When the witnesses lied —
(The FOURTH SPECTATOR *closely followed by the* FIFTH SPECTATOR *enters up left, and comes to slightly up centre.)*

Fourth Spectator. And friend denied his friend —

Fifth Spectator. When the cocklight cried.

First Spectator. All these years to the day since the temple veil —

Second Spectator. Was shrieked into ribbons while thunder and hail —

Third Spectator. Fanged the teeth of a gale —

Fourth Spectator. And hammer and nail —

Fifth Spectator. Told their terrible tale —

First Spectator. All these years to the day long gone, and yet —

Second Spectator *(crossing to right centre).* We still remember the ache and the fret —

Third Spectator. Of the cross growing wet —

Fourth Spectator (crossing down centre). With his blood and his sweat.

Fifth Spectator (coming down slightly right of FOURTH SPECTATOR). How could we forget?

(The crowd stays perfectly still. The MOTHER enters up left, and crosses down left.)

Mother. How could anyone forget? All these years to the day since my son died. I remember it as if it were yesterday. I remember his last week as if it had only just gone by. And such things happened in that week: my world was upturned, my life was blighted, my happiness broken for ever. Listen, and I will tell you. It began one night of storm when I dreamed a dream that my son was in great danger. I woke cold and frightened knowing I had to find him and warn him. But where should I make for? Where should I go? All I had heard was that Jesus was near to Jerusalem so that is where I went. As I came to the city I found myself among great crowds of people. (The SPECTATORS begin to arrange themselves as if they are watching a procession going by right—the FOURTH and FIFTH SPECTATORS keeping themselves somewhat apart from the others.) Some of them had cut branches from the trees, and they waved them, and they shouted as they watched a procession going by.

First Spectator. Here they are !

Second Spectator. That's him on the donkey !

Third Spectator. Blessings on him who comes in the name of the Lord !

Second Spectator. Hosanna to the King of Israel !

Fourth Spectator (to FIFTH SPECTATOR). Why does he come on a donkey?

Fifth Spectator. Some people will do anything to draw attention to themselves.

Fourth Spectator. I should have thought at least he would have used a chariot.

Fifth Spectator. That is what conquerors always use.

Fourth Spectator. Is he a conqueror ?

Fifth Spectator. The common people seem to think so.

Fourth Spectator. The common people will think anything they are told to think.

Fifth Spectator. He came up from nothing, you know: a carpenter from Nazareth, I believe. Well, really ! Nazareth, I ask you ! What good ever came out of there ?

Other Spectators. Hosanna !

Mother. Who is it you are cheering ?

First Spectator. The prophet, of course !

Second Spectator. Jesus of Nazareth !

Third Spectator. The prophet from Galilee !

Mother. Then I have found him.

Fifth Spectator. As far as we're concerned you can have him.

Fourth Spectator. We have rather more serious things to think about. *(As they go out up left).* Now, as to this little dinner party I am giving —

Mother. *(crossing to the other* SPECTATORS, *looking at the procession).* Yes, it is them. I must speak to them. *(She tries to push past them.)*

First Spectator. Here, here, who are you shoving ?

Second Spectator. Are you trying to push us out ?

Third Spectator. We've been here since dawn let me tell you.

First Spectator. Look, any more from you, and you'll feel the back edge of my hand. *(Shouts piously in the direction of the procession.)* Hail to the Prince of Peace !

Mother. Please let me through —

Second Spectator. Yes, any more of your shoving, and I'll blacken your eye for you. *(Shouts piously)* Good will towards all men !

Mother. Please —

Third Spectator. Keep back, can't you? Go and find your own pitch. *(Shouts piously)*   Everybody, love your neighbor !

All Three Spectators. Hosanna !

Mother. *(crossing to left.)* So they wouldn't let me through, and I couldn't get to my son. I just had to watch him go by in the procession with the crowd all cheering and shouting, and barring my path. Remember that crowd, won't you? Listen how they cheer the man on the donkey, and those who were with him. Listen, listen again.

The Spectators. *(beginning to turn).* Hosanna! Hosanna! Hosanna !

Mother. You will hear an echo of that later on.

The Spectators. *(now turning further; quieter.)* Hosanna. Hosanna. Hosanna.

Mother. Remember !

The Spectators. *(with backs to audience; a whisper.)* Hosanna. Hosanna. Hosanna. *(They go out.)*

Mother. So the procession had gone, and all I could do was to follow behind in the hope that somehow I could get through to my son. *(She goes out up right. The TEMPLE TRADER comes in, up left, carrying a basket over her shoulder. She comes down centre, and puts the basket on the ground.)*

Temple Trader. Am I a Pharisee? No! A Scribe? No! A Roman invader? Three times no! Then what am I? Tell me that. In all honesty tell me. No—don't tell me: I'll tell you. I'm a self-respecting, law-abiding, single-dealing, temple trader: that's what I am. As honest a

body as ever set up stall in the shadow of Solomon's Porch. And what's happened to me? Go on tell me: what *has* happened to me? No—don't tell me: I'll tell you. I was standing behind my stall just as I always do, minding my own business, shewing off my wares, getting on good terms with everybody with a Goodmorning here, and a Good Fortune there, and a Don't handle the goods, you little horror, here, there, and everywhere, when suddenly it come upon me. Yes, there in the Temple I was upturned, upset, toppled over, and otherwise capsized. One minute standing foursquare to the world on my own two feet: the next not knowing whether I was on my head or my elbow, surrounded by the finest assortment of squashed pomegranates, raisins, figcakes and apricots that money could buy. And my doves! My lovely little doves! All broke out of their cages, and going up and down the heavens like a ladderful of Jacob's angels. And it wasn't only the likes of me, you know. Oh no! The money changers come in for it as well. Up went their tables, down went their trays, and spondulicks from all over the world was swilling like a river across the courtyard. And who did it? Why, this young madman that's come among us: that's who did it. I never saw anyone so mad in all my life, and I've come across a few cranks in my time—but nothing like this one. I tell you, you don't catch me going anywhere near the temple while he's around: it wouldn't be safe. *(Moving down right.)* Do you know he said we were making it like a robber's cave. *(Turning.)* Well, I ask you: do I look like a robber? A brigand? More like a beggar now I'm forced to trade in the streets like this. *(Enter the* WIDOW *up left.)*
Fig cakes, lady?
(The WIDOW *shakes her head as she comes down left centre.)*
Raisins or pomegranates?
(Another shake of the head by the WIDOW.*)*
What about a nice juicy apricot then?

Widow. No, really, nothing thank you.

Temple Trader. Well you're not much good for trade, and that's a fact.

Widow. I'm sorry, but I've no money. I've given it all away—all that I had that is—though to be truthful you wouldn't have thought it very much.

Temple Trader. How much?

Widow. Just a mite or two, that's all.

Temple Trader. And that was all you had?

Widow. Yes.

Temple Trader. And you gave it all away?

Widow. Yes.

Temple Trader. Well, cheer up then, you're not much poorer by it; and come to that whoever you gave it to is not much richer either.

Widow. I gave it to the Temple.

Temple Trader. The Temple? You've come from there? Tell me: the madman: is he still around?

Widow. Which madman?

Temple Trader. The Nazarene, of course. Him who turned me off my pitch.

Widow. Yes, he was there. He saw me put the money in the chest. I was in the queue behind some merchants who were handing in bagfuls of shekels, and when it came to my turn, he pointed me out, and said that I had given more than any of the others.

Temple Trader. There, doesn't that just prove he's mad? And he's still up there, you say?

Widow. No, he has gone now—to Bethany, I believe. But I heard someone tell a poor woman who was asking for him that he would be back in town for the Passover.

Temple Trader. Then it's safe for me to go up there again to see what's happened to my pitch. That's the best bit of news I've had today. Here, here's a loaf of passover bread for you.

Widow. But I've no money.

Temple Trader. That's all right. It's free. *(Picking up her basket.)* Free! I must be going as mad as he is. *(She goes out down right.)*

Widow. *(quietly.)* I tell you this, he said, this poor widow has given more than any of the others for they gave only some of what they had, but she gave all that she had to live on. *(She holds up the bread as if asking a blessing.)* Let the passover be filled with good things, O God, for I who have nothing, and for he who saw how rich that nothing is. *(She goes out down left.)*
(The SERVANT *enters, up right, with a small stool which she places centre, and a besom with which she proceeds to sweep down left centre. The* MISTRESS *comes in, up right.)*

Mistress. Have the gentlemen all they require?

Servant. Yes, mistress.

Mistress. *(sitting.)* Enough food and drink?

Servant. Bread and wine for thirteen, mistress.

Mistress. There is something special about this party. Your master was most concerned we do everything for them. He is not even charging them for the use of the room.

Servant. And this afternoon he did a strange thing. He told me not to carry any water in the pitcher. He said he'd do it himself. Whoever heard of a man carrying water? That's woman's work. *(Sweeps.)*

Mistress. Well, your master knows best, I suppose. Men always do or so they tell us; and who are we to dispute them?

Servant. *(crossing to* MISTRESS.*)* I hope the master does know what he's doing. We've always had the reputation for being one of the best places. Some of this party—well, they're not exactly out of the top drawer, are they?

Mistress. I must agree I was a little surprised when I saw them go up the outer stair. Some of them looked even rougher than I thought they would.

Servant. And there wasn't half a row going on up there just now, I can tell you; about who was to be chief among them.

Mistress. But surely that is this Jesus of Nazareth —

Servant. It sounded as if he was going away.

Mistress. Well, that'll be good news for some.

Servant. Excuse me, mistress. *(Going up left and looking up as if responding to a call from the top of some stairs. The* MISTRESS *rises.)* Did you call, sir? A basin of water, sir, and a towel? Oh, certainly, sir. Right away, sir.

Mistress. What are they up to now?

Servant. I don't know, mistress, but I expect we'll soon find out. *(Calls.)* Coming, sir. *(She goes out up left.)*

Mistress. *(going down right.)* Well, they can't do much harm with water and a towel. In fact some of them look as if they could do themselves a bit of good with it. I only wish my husband had not got himself in with this outlandish lot. We were getting on very well. Making a nice little profit. Working up a nice little business, in fact. It's not going to do us any good being mixed up with such people as this. It could damage our reputation, and in the catering line reputation is everything. *(The* SERVANT *comes back up left.)* Well, what are they doing?

Servant. They're a strange crew and no mistake. Do you know what's happening now? He's washing their feet.

Mistress. *(crossing centre.)* Washing their feet? Who is?

Servant. This Jesus is.

Mistress. But he's supposed to be their leader.

Servant. Well, that's what he's doing, mistress. I saw him at it. There was a bit of a barney when he got to the big fellow but in the end he had to give in. Oh, they're a strange lot and no mistake. *(A sound of footsteps off left.)*

Mistress. Listen !

Servant. *(looking off left.)* Someone's coming down the stairs.

Mistress. *(joining SERVANT.)* It's one of them: he's going up the street.

Servant. Which one is it?

Mistress. I can't see. He's keeping well in the shadows whoever it is.

Servant. Well, at least we know one thing about him, mistress.

Mistress. What's that?

Servant. We know his feet are clean. *(They laugh, and go out up left. The MOTHER comes in up right and comes down right centre.)*

Mother. I was not finding it easy to meet up with my son. I could not keep up with the procession: the crowds were so great, you see, and I became so tired I had to give up, and come to the city in my own slow time. And when I got here how was I to find out where he was? Just a word here, a hint there — *(The MISTRESS and SERVANT come back up left.)* I am looking for Jesus of Nazareth and his followers. I was told they might be here.

Mistress. *(crossing centre.)* You are too late. He has gone. They have all gone.

Mother. Where did they go? I must find them.

Mistress. We have to be careful, you understand —

Mother. Would I harm my own son?

Mistress. They did not tell us where they were going. But we did overhear something. They have gone to the Garden of Gethsemane.

Mother. Where is that?

Mistress. Why, near the Mount of Olives, of course; surely you know of it?

Mother. No—no—how do I get there?

Servant. I can shew her if you like, mistress. I shall go home that way.

Mistress. There you are then. Go with her.

Mother. *(crossing to* SERVANT.*)* Take me quickly, please.

Servant. Good night, then, mistress. *(She goes out down left.)*

Mistress. Good night. Don't be late in the morning.

Mother. *(to* MISTRESS.*)* Thank you. *(She follows* SERVANT *down left.)*

Mistress. Good night. *(The* MOTHER *and the* SERVANT *go out.)* Well, I hope that's the last we hear of that lot. *(She picks up the stool and goes out up left. There is music. After a pause the* ANGELS *come in up right and up left and come down right and down left.)*

First Angel. Here is a pleasant garden.

Second Angel. By day it is cool—

First Angel. And dressed in the green corduroy of the trees.

Second Angel. By night it is secret—

First Angel. And cloaked with the velvet of midnight—

Second Angel. And filled with the silence of stars.

First Angel. It is a place of angels—

Second Angel. And they come here soft as shadows—

First Angel. To fill the air with murmurings—

Second Angel. For those with the ears to hear them.

First Angel. *We* are the angels.

Second Angel. *We* are the thoughts of God.

First Angel. We stand here guardians of the garden—

Second Angel. Waiting for God to come.

First Angel. Jesus: it is quiet tonight here in the garden. Only the buzzing of late insects, and the drift of the falling dew will you hear when you come.

Second Angel. Your robe will brush aside the praying grasses, and your knees print the ground like the nests of larks when you speak to the Father.

First Angel. Come Jesus, and pray your last long prayer here where it seems but an ordinary night with ordinary things happening in the unsuspecting town. Man and maid still love under the stars; the coarse tavern jests rip through the tippled night; and the shepherd still staves his flocks on the fleecy plain. To them it is an ordinary night, though only you know it is not ordinary. It is the testing time of the world, but the world does not know the test.

Second Angel. He comes, and the others with him.

First Angel. All except the one.

Second Angel. Yes, all except the one.

First Angel. *His* time to come is not yet.

Second Angel. Jesus leaves the others. He is coming to pray.

First Angel. The others will watch.

Second Angel. The others will sleep.

First Angel. All except the one.

Second Angel. Yes, all except the one.

First Angel. Jesus prays. Listen.

Second Angel. *(crossing to* FIRST ANGEL *slowly before she speaks.)* Father, he says, if it be thy will—

First Angel. Take this cup from me.

Second Angel. Yet not my will but thine be done.

First Angel. Look at the anguish.

Second Angel. The agony.

First Angel. The sweat.

Second Angel. The blood.

First Angel. The long storm of prayer.

Second Angel. The great silence of supplication.

First Angel. The garden is at peace again.

Second Angel. The others sleep.

First Angel. All except the one.

Second Angel. Yes, all except the one. *(She goes slowly back to down right again. The* MOTHER *and the* SERVANT *come in up left and move to up centre.)*

Servant. This is the place.

Mother. It is quiet here.

Servant. They say angels are supposed to come here, but I've never seen any.

Mother. *(looking about her.)* It's so dark it's difficult to see anything.

Servant. Some men are sleeping over there.

Mother. *(peering and pointing down left.)* And that one seems to be praying.

Servant. *(crossing quickly, down left.)* And look: torch-light! Why, it's soldiers! What are they doing here?

Mother. And—and—there's my son! I'm sure it is. What is happening?

Servant. It's that Jesus of Nazareth: they're taking him away.

Mother. What does it mean? What does it mean? *(She runs out followed by the* SERVANT, *down left.)*

First Angel. Here is a pleasant garden.

(Soft music.)

Second Angel. By day it is cool—

First Angel. *(crossing to right.)* And dressed in the green corduroy of the trees.

Second Angel. By night it is secret—

First Angel. And filled with the silence of stars. *(They go out down right. After exit music the* KITCHEN-WOMAN *carrying a brazier comes in up right. She moves down right, and puts down the brazier.)*

Kitchenwoman. Well, here we are then at the High
Priest's House. Old Caiaphas. Old Frosty Face. Old
Puff and Blow. Old Spit and Beard. I've got all sorts
of names for him. I could go on all night if you wanted
me to. But he's not a bad old lad really, I suppose. After
all you expect a High Priest to be a bit stuck up, don't
you? You've got to have a bit of the old lahdidah when
you get up in the world. Besides in the long run it does
me a bit of good too. All the others are a bit envious of me
like: personal kitchenwoman to the High Priest. Well,
what do you think about things, eh? I suppose you've
heard the news. They've brought in The Nazarene.
Got him last night up in Gethsemane. One of his mates
sold him out, I believe. Got the usual cut of thirty pieces,
I suppose. Funny really, 'cause this lot wasn't supposed
to worry overmuch about money. But it just goes to shew.
In the end, money always talks. Here, it's a bit of a cold
one tonight, isn't it? A good job they told me to get this
fire going—we'd be froze stiff without it. D'you see the
Nazarene over there? *(Pointing left.)* Not much of a world
beater about him is there? Not when you see him stripped
off like that. Come closer to the fire if you're cold.
(Looking right) Yes, that means you as well, Big Fellow.
Here, here, haven't I seen you before? Come on now, yes I
have, yes I have. You were with the Nazarene surely.
Yes you were! What's that? You're not denying it, are
you? Well, you may be right. But I could have sworn —
(The FIRST *and* SECOND SPECTATORS *come
down left.)*

First Spectator *(pointing right.)* That one: what's he
doing here? He was with the man Jesus. I'm sure he was.

Kitchenwoman. Well, now, haven't I just been saying
the same thing?

First Spectator. *(crossing to right centre followed by*
SECOND SPECTATOR.*)* Listen to him, All right. All
right. There's no need for all that swearing. If you don't
know him we'll take your word for it.

Second Spectator. I don't know if I believe him. Hark at the way he talks. Come on now: let's have a straight answer to a straight question: do you or don't you know this man Jesus? *(The sound of cock-crow.)*

Kitchenwoman. Well that's plain enough. All right. You don't know him. We believe you. You needn't slink off, you know. We're sorry and all that; but you can't be too careful, can you?

Second Spectator. Do you see that? He's crying. A big fellow like that.

First Spectator. Just because we got on to him a bit.

Kitchenwoman. He's not the only one. Look at the Nazarene over there. He's shedding a few too. Well, come on. *(Lifting the brazier and crossing to down left.)* I think we'll move over under the archways: it won't be quite so raw over there. *(Resting brazier.)* Don't you worry, Nazarene: you won't be cold much longer. You haven't got long to wait now. You'll be a lot warmer in the place where you're going. *(She lifts the brazier again and goes out down left followed by the SPECTATORS. The MOTHER comes in up left.)*

Mother. *(crossing down left.)* Such things have happened since the last time I saw my son that evil night in the garden. Such terrible things. Such trouble. Such pain. And now I have come to this temple to see the prophetess I have been told about. *(The PROPHETESS, carrying a scroll, enters up left and crosses slowly to right.)* Perhaps she will tell me what has happened to my son. *(Moving to up centre to meet the PROPHETESS.)* Great Prophetess: I have been told to seek you out, to ask comfort from you. *(The MOTHER kneels and touches the robe of the PROPHETESS.)*

Prophetess. *(with a motion of blessing.)* What is troubling you, daughter?

Mother. I am trying to find my son. You know of Jesus of Nazareth?

Prophetess. Who does not know of him? He is an enemy of the people. He has been arrested.

Mother. So it was he they took in the garden. Where is he now?

Prophetess. Somewhere between Herod, The High Priest and Pilate, I suppose.

Mother. What are they doing to him?

Prophetess. *(turning away and moving down right centre.)* They are trying him, of course. He will be condemned. He will be crucified. Then we shall see how great he is. In a little while he will be gone, his remembrance shall perish from the earth, and he shall have no name in the street. You will see.

Mother. But he is good—

Prophetess. *(turning towards the* MOTHER). He is a revolutionary, a blasphemer. *(Going down right.)* There is only one way of dealing with such people. They must be destroyed or else, you see, they destroy us. It is as simple as that. There is nothing personal about this, you understand. It is simply a matter of theological necessity.

Mother. What of his friends?

Prophetess. They scattered themselves very quickly when the hour came. They made sure they weren't there when it struck. They went as fast as their legs could carry them. All except the one. The one who led us to him. *(The* KITCHENWOMAN *comes running in up left.)*

Kitchenwoman. Here's a queer thing. You know the chap what sold out the Nazarene? I just passed him in the street, slouching along in the shadows, rolling about as if he'd taken a drop too much, and crying his eyes out, and carrying his bag of silver still with him. *(Looking off down left.)* Here, what's happening out there? Look it's him! What's he doing? Hey, look out! *(A bag of coins from left is thrown across the* *stage.)* What do you think you're doing, Iscariot, throwing your money around like this?

Mother. Did you say Iscariot?

Kitchenwoman. That's right, lady, Judas Iscariot.

Mother. Not Judas! No, not Judas! No! *(She goes down left.)*

Kitchenwoman. Did I say something? *(Shouting after the* MOTHER.*)* It's a fact all right. He's the one that spilled the beans. Begging your pardon, Prophetess. *(She goes out down left.)*

Prophetess. *(picking up a bag of money.)* Well, we can always find a use for it, I suppose. *(As she goes out down right.)* There was some talk of the Potter's Field coming into the market — *(She has gone out. The* FIRST *and* SECOND SPECTATORS *come back followed by the* THIRD.*)*

First Spectator. What I heard was this: that Pilate has seen him and sent him on to Herod.

Second Spectator. You're out of date. Herod saw him all right then pitched him back to Pilate.

Third Spectator. After he'd had a bit of fun with him. They say he sent him back to Pilate dressed in a gorgeous robe of purple.

Second Spectator. That's right enough. See for yourself.

Third Spectator. *(moving down left.)* Poor chap—he looks all in. *(The others join her in a group down left. All look up as if towards a balcony, left.)*

First Spectator. So would you be if you were being tried before the Governor for your life. What does Pilate say?

Second Spectator. Are you the King of the Jews?

Third Spectator. Answer up, Nazarene!

First Spectator. I can't hear him.

Third Spectator. He says the words are yours.

First Spectator. What does Pilate say to that?

Second Spectator. He finds no fault in him.

First Spectator. No fault in him?

Second Spectator. He wants to let him off with a flogging.

Third Spectator. Don't let him get away with it, Pilate.

Second Spectator. He's an enemy of the people.

First Spectator. What will Caesar say if you let him go?

All Three. Kill him, Pilate, kill him!

First Spectator. What about the privilege, Pilate?

Third Spectator. Yes, what about it?

First Spectator. What's that he says?

Second Spectator. We can have Jesus or Barabbas.

Third Spectator. Barabbas or Jesus.

First Spectator. Then give us Barabbas!

Second Spectator. Yes, Barabbas!

Third Spectator. Barabbas!

All Three. Barabbas! *(The FIRST ANGEL comes in, up right, and the SECOND ANGEL, down right.)*

First Angel. Was it less than a week ago? Do you remember these very same people when the man on the donkey rode past?

Second Angel. Do you remember their voices raised in the praise of the moment as he and his friends went by?

First Angel. Listen again!

Second Angel. Listen.

(The SPECTATORS turn towards the front.)

First Spectator. Hosanna!

Second Spectator. Hosanna!

Third Spectator. Hosanna!

All Three. Hosanna!

First Angel. But now it has become—
(The SPECTATORS *turn back to look at the balcony again.)*

First Spectator. Barabbas!

Second Spectator. Barabbas!

Third Spectator. Barabbas!

All Three. Barabbas!

Second Angel. Well, you can have your Barabbas if you want him.

First Spectator. He's going to release Barabbas!

Second Spectator. Jesus is to die!

Third Spectator. Death to the Nazarene!

First Spectator. We have won!

Second Spectator. A victory for common sense!

Third Spectator. A victory for justice!

First Spectator. See you up at the hill. *(She goes off, up left.)*

Second Spectator. Try and keep me away. *(She follows, up left.)*

Third Spectator. Death to all traitors! *(She goes out down left.)*

First Angel. *(crossing to down left before she speaks.)* There is a hill outside the city where in the cool of summer evenings people come and look out over the streets and houses, and are proud to belong to such a splendid place.

Second Angel. They talk and laugh here. In moments of joy they feel themselves so near to heaven they almost reach up and take a handful of early stars from the evening sky. In moments of sadness they come here alone to bury their griefs in the tombs of the darkening night.

First Angel. It is a merry meeting place when the city is alight with holiday, when people are free to tune the airs of the wind with jests, when laughter is carried to the little clouds of summer as if plucked from the strings of a thousand harps.

Second Angel. It is also a place where people come to see others put to death. It is the place where they set up crosses in their dreary season.

First Angel. It is the place of execution.

Second Angel. The place of the dead.

First Angel. The place of the skull.

Second Angel. They are coming today the crowds. *(The* THREE SPECTATORS *come in up left and form a group up right.)* You can hear them. You can see them. They will come as if to a wedding feast. They will shout with joy. They will be exalted. They will be filled with the excitement of life.

First Angel. For men are to be done to death today in this prominent and varied place.

Third Spectator. *(indicating down right.)* They're puting the three of them up together.

First Spectator. You crowned him with spiky thorns, soldier!

Second Spectator. You made him carry the cross, soldier!

Third Spectator. Now drive the nails in hard, soldier!

All Three. For this is the king of the Jews!
(The TEMPLE TRADER *runs in from up left carrying a wineskin, crosses down right centre, and looks up as if at the cross.)*

Temple Trader. Look, that's what they've writ up over him: King of the Jews. Who'd have thought my old friend the madman would have rose up so high in the world? *(To the audience and spectators.)* Did you hear that? My old friend! Well, why not? Look at the good he's done me today. Brought the biggest crowd here since we strung up the caravan robbers, and that must be five years or more agone now. And I'm cleaned out, bought up, all goods disposed of, and otherwise sold out. And all thanks to him! And tomorrow back at the old pitch: Stall 22, shadow of Solomon's Porch. You know where to find me *(turning towards the cross again.)* And *you* won't be turning me over again in a hurry, and that's a fact. No, by the look of things somebody's been turning you over for a change, and I must say you don't seem so good on it.

Second Spectator. Hey, he's thirsty, centurion!

First Spectator. Yes, give him a drink!

Third Spectator. Go on: give him some water.

Temple Trader. I got something better than that for him! A skinful of wine for His Majesty! A little bit sour it's true—returned to stock, unfit for human consumption—but just about do for him though. Here you are, soldier, send him up a spongeful of this on the end of your spear. After all, one good turn deserves another! *(She goes out, down right.)*

First Spectator. It's getting dark.

Second Spectator. We're in for a storm. *(Sound of distant thunder.)*

First Angel. Thunder.

Second Angel. Lightning.

First Angel. Darkness.

Second Angel. Rain.

Second Spectator. The earth—it trembles.

First Angel. Well may it tremble as it feels the agony of its darkest hour—

Second Angel. The agony of its greatest spirit—

First Angel. Come to its end in the poor broken body of an outraged man.

Second Angel. Listen; he speaks.

First Spectator. What's he saying?

First Angel. He says: Father into thy hands I commit my spirit. *(A sound of thunder; through which the* TEMPLE TRADER *is heard calling derisively "King of the Jews!" a cry that fades into the distance strangely echoing the cockcrow that we heard earlier.)*

First Spectator. *(kneeling.)* It is all over.

Second Spectator. *(kneeling.)* Have we done right?

Third Spectator. *(kneeling.)* Perhaps he was indeed the king of the Jews.

Second Angel. *(with irony.)* Hosanna!

First Angel. *(with irony.)* Hosanna!

Together. Hosanna! *(They go out down right and left.)*

First Spectator. We sorrow here at the foot of the cross.

Second Spectator. We see the poor battered body of Jesus.

Third Spectator. And we are sorry that we and our kind have caused such pain at the end of a human life.

First Spectator. For we ourselves are human.

Second Spectator. Yes, that is our excuse--

Third Spectator. We are human.

First Spectator. We try to be true to a pattern.

Second Spectator. But there is something that sometimes prevents us.

Third Spectator. It is the unknown factor—

First Spectator. The mysterious equation—

Second Spectator. The flaw in the casting—

Third Spectator. That some call human nature.
(The SPECTATORS *rise.)*

First Spectator. This man was a good man.

Second Spectator. He forged his pattern and was true to it.

Third Spectator. So perhaps that is why we destroyed him.

First Spectator. For while he lived he was a conscience ever before us.

Second Spectator. But now that he is dead perhaps we can go on as we did before.

Third Spectator. Yet I have a strange feeling—

First Spectator. That this is only the beginning—

Third Spectator. That by his death that conscience will grow stronger than ever.

Second Spectator. That we will be more disturbed as time goes on.

First Spectator. That the world will be more disturbed as time goes on.

(The MOTHER *comes in down left, crosses to kneel right centre and looks out towards the cross.)*

Mother. I too am broken, Jesus. I kneel at the foot of your cross and sorrow, a mother weeping for her son. Forgive us all our shortcomings, Jesus.

(The WIDOW *comes in down left.)*

Widow. So you have found your son at last?

Mother. No, this is not my son, except insofar as he is every woman's son from this time out. No, my son was another. A little boy who grew up to be strong, and to love his country, and who did all he did for pure love of that country. No, I am the mother of Judas the betrayer. *(The others recoil.)* All you who draw away: are you not betrayers too? *(To the audience.)* All you who are gathered here: is there not some of Judas in your hearts? And when you count the change in your purses or chink the coins in your pockets, can you be sure there are not some pieces of tainted silver among them? Pray, pray, pray that you are never brought to the test.

First Spectator. All these years to the day long gone, and yet—

Second Spectator. We still remember the ache and the fret—

Third Spectator. Of the cross growing wet—

Widow. With his blood and his sweat. *(She goes out down left.)*

First Spectator. How could we forget? *(She goes out up left.)*

Second Spectator. How could we forget? *(She goes out up right.)*

Third Spectator. How could we forget? *(She goes out down left.)*

Mother. *(to the audience.)* How can you forget?

CURTAIN

PRODUCTION NOTES

Casting. As already stated at the beginning, the play may be performed by casts of from eight to fourteen players. For a cast of eight the characters may be shared like this:

Player 1 takes First Spectator and Mistress;
Player 2 takes Second Spectator and Servant;
Player 3 takes Third Spectator and Kitchenwoman;
Player 4 takes Fourth Spectator, Temple Trader and Prophetess;
Player 5 takes Fifth Spectator and Widow;
Player 6 takes The Mother;
Player 7 takes First Angel;
Player 8 takes Second Angel.

For larger casts the doubled parts are given to the extra players as available.

For the first Church performance The Concord Society of Uxbridge performed the play with a mixed cast. They allocated the following parts to men in their very successful production: First Spectator, Third Spectator, Fifth Spectator, Temple Trader, and Prophetess (calling the character a Priest.)

Set. This is a simple play to stage, and it may be performed in a curtain set—using a skycloth if available—with no furnishings whatsoever. If the stage is large enough then the acting area should be loosely defined by some half a dozen blocks of a variety of shapes and sizes which are quite easily made from cardboard boxes, and painted a neutral color.

Lighting. The play may be performed in straight lighting. If special effects are available they can greatly help the atmosphere by softening the limits of the acting area, and so prevent the sharp cut-off of exits and entrances into and from the wings. Thus the characters that the audience sees have the strongest possible links with the ones that they do not see off-stage. Pools of light should be arranged to cover the main acting areas, and their intensity should be adjusted as the grouping shifts. General lighting should not be too bright, and its color varied to suit the mood of the scenes. In the Garden Scene the Angels are lit by green floods from the wings.

The light on the backcloth should be dimmed just before the thunderstorm, and later lightning flashed on to it at appropriate places.

During the entire scene at the foot of the cross a single flood from the right wing or from F.O.H. should light the faces of the Spectators, and later the face of The Mother. This light together with the backcloth light are the only ones left at the end.

Costumes: BIBLICAL COSTUME by Marion Wright (published by S.P.C.K.) is useful. The costumes of the crowd should, of course, blend for color—the Fourth and Fifth Spectators being better dressed than the rest of them. The Temple Trader should wear vivid colors; the Widow black; and the Prophetess may wear silk. The Mother's costume should contrast with the rest without being too striking. The Angels should be draped in shiny pale blue-grey material — their heads covered—and they should not wear wings.

Acting. The production of the play must, of course, be stylized to a certain extent, and symbolic movement should be used when appropriate—for example in the thunderstorm scene. When characters have to address the audience they should do so deliberately, taking the audience into their confidence—there should be nothing half-hearted about it. The grouping of the three main spectators has been designed assuming that the First is the tallest and the Third the smallest: adjustment will have to be made if this is not so.

Properties. Most of the properties—and there are not many—are easily made or come by. The Temple Trader's basket is sufficiently small for her to carry over her shoulder yet large enough to hold a reasonable stock of goods. The wineskin which she brings in for her second scene is made from velour material suitably padded out. The Kitchenwoman's brazier may be adapted from a grid type of garden incinerator with torchlight under red paper to furnish the fire. Another form of brazier may be made by punching holes in the side of an old bucket, and letting the fire shine through these.

Music. You may find the choral music of Tomas Luis Victoria—of which several recordings have been made—useful as introductory and incidental music. **The Lamentations of Jeremiah** which was especially written for Maundy Thursday is especially recommended.

THE LAST BLUE MOUNTAIN

For one man and three women. A plane has crashed and there are only three survivors one of whom is dying. The others think they recognise him but cannot call to mind who he is. In his delirium he goes back to the most poignant moments of his life. We learn that he was a world-famous conductor of a great orchestra who left the woman he loved, forsook fame and acclamation, to seek the lost idealism and dreams of his youth. In a most dramatic and unusual sequence his past is linked with the present and he finds all the things he has been looking for just as a rescue party approaches to end the play. A contest winner of great atmosphere and beauty giving plenty of scope for dramatic acting with opportunities for using music and lighting effects if desired.

THE REVIVAL

An Improbable History in One Act with A Postscript for one man and two women. A simply staged, easily costumed, light-hearted play about Shakespeare in retirement.

"A credible and affectionate portrait of the great man in his later years"—*Amateur Stage, U.K.*

"A warm, witty, easy-to-stage play of high competition calibre"—*Baker's Plays, U.S.A.*

MURDER AT THE GREY'S HOUND MANSION
Maxine Holmgren

Mystery, High School/ Community Theatre / 5f, 3m / Simple Set
This is a mysterious comedy (or a comical mystery) that will have everyone howling with laughter.

The eccentric owner of Grey's Hound Mansion has been murdered. The cast gathers at the gloomy mansion for the reading of the will. Lightning lights up the stage as thunder and barking dogs greet the wacky characters that arrive. Each one is a suspect, and each one suspects another. Mixed metaphors and alliterations will have the audience barking up the wrong tree until the mystery is solved.

Baker's Plays
7611 Sunset Blvd.
Los Angeles, CA 90046
Phone: 323-876-0579
Fax: 323-876-5482

BAKERSPLAYS.COM

STONE SOUP
Anne Glasner & Betty Hollinger

Musical, TYA/Children's Theatre / 9m, 7f, 2 either / Simple Set
2 hungry soldiers stumble on a town filled with disgruntled neighbors. Using their imaginations, the soldiers trick the townsfolk into donating seasonings for their legendary Stone Soup, which they have convinced the townsfolk is a delicacy beyond measure. They con the townfolk into giving them all the ingredients to make a real soup, and in doing so, the soldiers help the townsfolk learn how to get along with each other by working together to create something good.

Baker's Plays
7611 Sunset Blvd.
Los Angeles, CA 90046
Phone: 323-876-0579
Fax: 323-876-5482

BAKERSPLAYS.COM

ELEANOR FOR PRESIDENT
Merritt Ierley

18+ m, 9+ f, ensemble (some gender flexibility and doubling possible)
A woman as Chief Executive? The 2008 presidential campaign proved it possible, yet it just might have happened more than half a century earlier. Eleanor Roosevelt, First Lady from 1933 to 1945, might have run for president after the death of her husband, Franklin. Many thought about it, some talked about it, a few actually suggested it. That Eleanor Roosevelt did not seek public office was of her own choosing, and chiefly her own priorities as well as a sense that the time was not yet right. Act I of Eleanor for President briefly scans her career to a point where she might have run. Act II fictionalizes the fork in the road not takes. The net result is a unique, sometimes witty, and always insightful look at Eleanor Roosevelt and the political process.

Baker's Plays
7611 Sunset Blvd.
Los Angeles, CA 90046
Phone: 323-876-0579
Fax: 323-876-5482

BAKERSPLAYS.COM

9 780874 401189